Sarah Daniel

AIR FRYER QUICK & EASY VOL. 2

EVERYDAY QUICK & EASY RECIPES FOR AIR FRYER LOVERS

Kensington Recipe Press

© 2021 Kensington Recipe Press - All rights reserved.

Photography Humbert Castillo
Graphic design Yuka Okuma
Editorial coordination Lizzie Martin

First edition March 2021

The following book is reproduced below to provide information that is as accurate and reliable as possible. Regardless, purchasing this book can be seen as consent because both the publisher and the author of this book are in no way experts on the topics discussed within. Any recommendations or suggestions that are made herein are for entertainment purposes only. Professionals should be consulted as needed before undertaking any of the actions endorsed herein. This declaration is deemed fair and valid by both the American Bar Association and the Committee of Publishers Association and is legally binding throughout the United States. Furthermore, the transmission, duplication, or reproduction of any of the following work, including specific information, will be considered an illegal act irrespective of if it is done electronically or in print. This extends to creating a secondary or tertiary copy of the work or a recorded document and can only express written consent from the publisher. All additional rights reserved. The information in the following pages is broadly considered a truthful and accurate account of facts. As such, any inattention, use, or misuse of the information in question by the reader will render any resulting actions solely under their purview. There are no scenarios in which the publisher or the original author of this work can be in any fashion deemed liable for any hardship or damages that may befall them after undertaking the information described herein. Additionally, the following pages' information is intended only for informational purposes and should thus be thought of as universal. As befitting its nature, it is presented without assurance regarding its prolonged validity or interim quality. Trademarks that are mentioned are done without written consent and can in no way be considered an endorsement from the trademark holder.

Table of Content

QUICK & EASY RECIPES 10

- Pork Burger Cutlets 12
- Lamb Fries 14
- Barbecue Pork Club Sandwich 16
- Pork Burger Cutlets 18
- Tasty Kale and Celery Crackers 20
- Tuna Cakes 22
- Toasted Seasoned Nuts 24
- Nacho Coated Prawns 26
- Cheesy Mustard and Ham Rounds 28
- Grilled Cheese Delight 30
- Roti Prata Mini Sausage Rolls 32
- Filo Covered Apple Pie 34
- Puff Pastry Banana Rolls 36
- Crunchy Sweet Potato Sticks 38
- Spring Rolls 40
- Syrupy Buttered Figs with Mascarpone 42
- Corn Tortilla Chips 44
- Air Fried Banana Chips 46
- Rosemary Chips 48
- Air Fried Crab Sticks 50
- Bread Rolls with Crisp Potato Stuffing 52
- Feta and Onion Bell Pepper Rolls 54
- Spicy Coconut Coated Shrimp 56
- Crispy French Fries 58
- Bacon-Wrapped Shrimp 60
- Sage and Onion Stuffing Balls Air-Fryer 62
- Chenjehn 64
- Juicy Kebab 66
- Banana Rolls 68
- Milanese Of Eggplant 70
- Uruguayan Fried Cakes 72
- Delicious Malanga 74
- Artichoke Croquettes 76
- Caramelized Bananas 78
- Banana Pie 80
- Fried Vegan Milk 82
- Celery Fritters 84
- Vegan Donuts 86
- Andes Cakes 88

Eggplant with Garlic	90
Apple Fritters	92
Cinammon Apples	94
Fried Tofu	96
Vegan French Toast with Oregano	98
Vegan Chips	100
Vegetarian Pizza	102

Quick & Easy Recipes

Pork Burger Cutlets

Ready in about 35 min | Servings 2 | Normal

Ingredients:

- ½ lb. of pork (Make sure that you mince the pork fine)
- ½ cup of breadcrumbs
- A pinch of salt to taste
- ¼ teaspoon of ginger finely chopped
- 1 green chili finely chopped
- 1 teaspoon of lemon juice
- 1 tablespoon. of fresh coriander leaves. Chop them finely
- ¼ teaspoon of red chili powder
- ½ cup of boiled peas
- ¼ teaspoon of cumin powder
- ¼ teaspoon of dried mango powder

Directions:

1. Take a pot and add all the masalas, onions, green chilies, peas, cilantro leaves, lemon juice, ginger, and 1-2 tbsp into the breadcrumbs.
2. Add the sliced pork. I combine all the ingredients. Mold the mixture into Cutlets Round. Kindly press them back. Now scrupulously roll them out.
3. Preheat the Air Fryer for 5 minutes, at 250° F . Open the Fryer's box and place the Cutlets in the pan. Near gently.
4. Hold the fryer at about 10 to 12 minutes, at 150° F. Turn the Cutlets over in between the cooking process to get a standard dish. Serve sweet chutney with basil.

Lamb fries

Ready in about 40 min | Servings 2 | Normal

Ingredients:

- 1 lb. of boneless lamb cut into fingers
- 2 cup of dry breadcrumbs
- 2 teaspoon of oregano
- 2 teaspoon of red chili flakes
- For the Marinade:
- 1 ½ tbsp. of ginger-garlic paste
- 4 tablespoon of lemon juice
- 2 teaspoon of salt
- 1 teaspoon of pepper powder
- 1 teaspoon of red chili powder
- 6 tablespoon of cornflour
- 4 eggs

Directions:

1. Mix all the marinade ingredients, put the lamb's fingers inside, and let it rest overnight. Mix well the breadcrumbs, oregano, and red chili flakes, then placing the marinated fingers on the mixture.
2. Cover with plastic wrap and keep before just before starting food—prefire up the Air Fryer for 5 minutes at 160° F.
3. Place your fingers in and close the fry box. Let them cook for another 15 minutes at the same time, or so. Flip well the fingers until they are fried equally.

Barbecue Pork Club Sandwich

Ready in about 25 min | Servings 2 | Normal

Ingredients:

- 2 slices of white bread
- 1 tablespoon of softened butter
- ½ lb. of cut pork (Get the meat cut into cubes)
- 1 small capsicum

For Barbeque Sauce:

- ¼ tablespoon of Worcestershire sauce
- ½ teaspoon of olive oil
- ½ flake of garlic crushed
- ¼ cup of chopped onion
- ¼ teaspoon of mustard powder
- ½ tablespoon of sugar
- ¼ tablespoon of red chili sauce
- 1 tablespoon of tomato ketchup
- ½ cup of water.

Directions:

1. Take the bread slices and cut the rims. Still cut horizontally on the strips. Heat the sauce ingredients and wait before the sauce thickens. Now apply the pork to the sauce and whisk before the flavors are acquired.

2. Whisk the capsicum and scrape off the flesh. The capsicum is sliced into strips. Mix the ingredients, and add them to the slices of bread.

3. Preheat theAir Fryer about 300° F for 5 minutes. Open the Fryer's basket and put the cooked sandwiches in it, ensuring that no two sandwiches meet each other. Hold the fryer at about 15 minutes now at 250°

4. Switch the sandwiches to cook both slices in between the cooking process. Serve the strawberry ketchup or mint chutney sandwiches.

Pork Burger Cutlets

Ready in about 30 min | Servings 2 | Normal

Ingredients:

- ½ lb. of pork (Make sure that you mince the pork fine)
- ½ cup of breadcrumbs
- A pinch of salt to taste
- ¼ teaspoon of ginger finely chopped
- 1 green chili finely chopped
- 1 teaspoon of lemon juice
- 1 tablespoon of fresh coriander leaves. Chop them finely
- ¼ teaspoon of red chili powder
- ½ cup of boiled peas
- ¼ teaspoon of cumin powder
- ¼ teaspoon of dried mango powder

Directions:

1. Take a pot and add all the masalas, onions, green chilies, peas, cilantro leaves, lemon juice, ginger, and 1-2 tablespoon into it. Breadcrumbs, crumbs. Then add the sliced pork.
2. Combine all the ingredients. Mold the mixture into Cutlets Round. Kindly press them back. Now scrupulously roll them out.
3. Preheat the Air Fryer for 5 minutes, at 250° F. Open the Fryer's box and place the Cutlets in the pan. Hold the fryer at about 10 to 12 minutes, at 150°F. Turn the Cutlets over in between the cooking process to get a classic dish. Serve nice with mint chutney.

Tasty Kale and Celery Crackers

Ready in about 30 min | Servings 6 | Normal

Ingredients:

- 2 cups of flaxseed, ground
- 2 cups of flax seed, soaked overnight and drained
- 4 bunches of kale, chopped
- 1 bunch of basil, chopped
- ½ bunch of celery, chopped
- 4 garlic cloves, minced
- 1/3 cup of olive oil

Directions:

1. Mix the ground flaxseed with the celery, kale, basil, and garlic in your food processor and mix well.
2. Add the oil and soaked flaxseed, then mix again, scatter in the pan of your Air Fryer, break into medium crackers and cook for 20 minutes at 380° F.
3. When the timer reaches 0, then press the cancel button
4. Serve as an appetizer and break into cups.

Enjoy!

Tuna Cakes

Ready in about 20 min | Servings 12 | Normal

Ingredients:

- 15 ounces of canned tuna, drain and flaked
- 3 eggs
- ½ teaspoon of dill, dried
- 1 teaspoon of parsley, dried
- ½ cup of red onion, chopped
- 1 teaspoon of garlic powder
- Salt and black pepper to the taste
- Cooking spray

Directions:

1. Mix the tuna with salt, pepper, dill, parsley, onion, garlic powder, and eggs in a cup, whisk well, and make medium cakes out of the mixture.
2. Place the tuna cakes in the basket of your Air Fryer, spray them with the cooking oil and cook for 10 minutes at 350° F and turn them halfway.
3. When the timer reaches 0, then press the cancel button
4. Place them on a tray and act as an appetizer.

Enjoy!

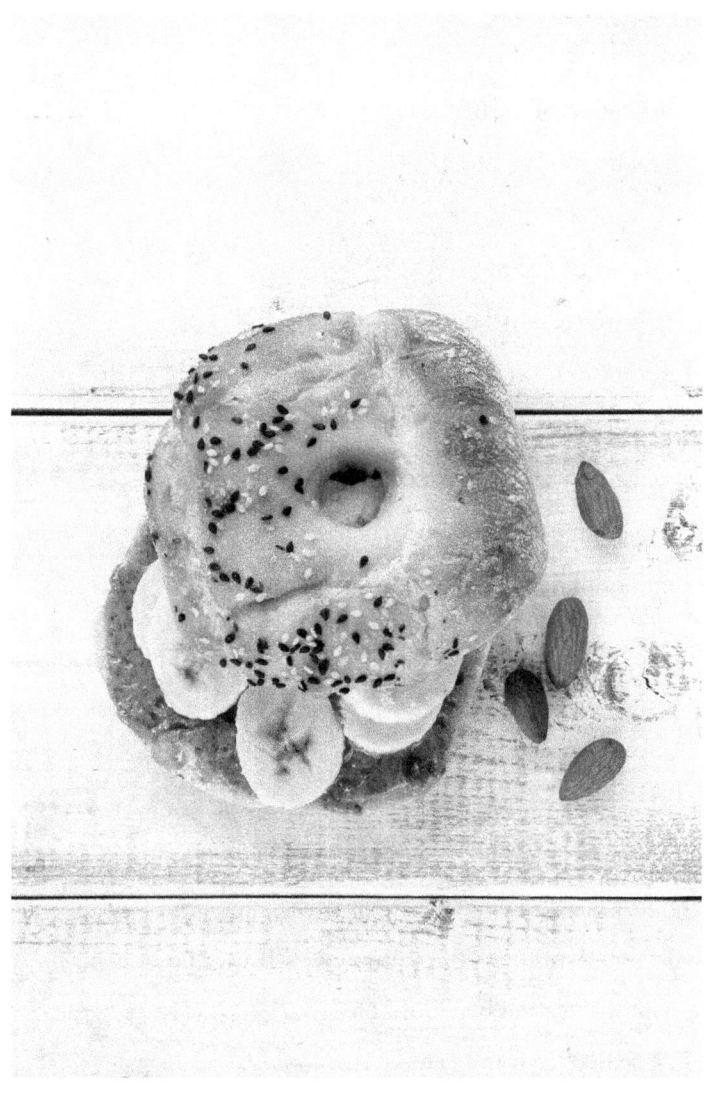

Toasted Seasoned Nuts

Ready in about 55 min | Servings 3 | Normal

Ingredients:

- ¼ teaspoon of garlic cloves, ground
- ½ pound of cashews
- 4 tablespoons of sugar
- 8 ounces of pecan halves
- 1 egg white, whisked
- 1 teaspoon of salt
- ½ teaspoon of cinnamon
- ¼ teaspoon of mixed spice
- ¼ teaspoon of cayenne pepper
- 1 cup of almonds

Directions:

1. Mix the sugar, garlic, mixed spice, pepper, salt, cinnamon, and egg in a bowl.
2. Select bake mode the set the temperature to heat your Air Fryer to 300°F.
3. Put the cashews, almonds, and pecan into the egg mixture and toss.
4. Coat the fryer basket with oil using a brush and pour half the nut mixture on it. Toast for 25 minutes until crunchy, stirring the nuts at intervals. Do the same with the second batch of nuts.
5. Store in a sealed jar if not eaten immediately.

Nacho Coated Prawns

Ready in about 30 min | Servings 3-4 | Normal

Ingredients:

- 9 ounces of nacho chips
- 1 egg, whisked
- 18 medium-sized prawns

Directions:

1. Remove the shell and veins from the prawns, wash thoroughly, and wipe dry.
2. Grind the chips in a bowl until pieces areas that of breadcrumbs.
3. Dip each prawn into the egg and then coat with the chip crumbs.
4. Select bake mode the set the temperature to heat the Air Fryer to 356° F.
5. Put the prawns into the Air Fryer and cook for 8 minutes. Serve with salsa or sour cream.

Cheesy Mustard and Ham Rounds

Ready in about 45 min | Servings 6 | Normal

Ingredients:

- 2 cups of Gruyere cheese, grated
- 6 slices of ham
- 1 tablespoon of mustard
- 1 sheet of pre-rolled puff pastry

Directions:

1. Cover your workbench with flour and put the pastry on it.
2. Add the ham, mustard, and cheese evenly on the pastry and roll up beginning from the shorter edge.
3. Cover with cling film and place in the freezer until firm for 30 minutes. Remove, and slice into 1cm thick small circles.
4. Select bake mode the set the temperature to heat your Air Fryer to 370° F and cook the rounds in it until golden brown for 10 minutes.

Grilled Cheese Delight

Ready in about 15 min | Servings 2 | Normal

Ingredients:

- 4 slices of white bread
- ¼ cup of butter, melted
- ½ cup of sharp cheddar cheese

Directions:

1. Select bake mode the set the temperature to preheat the Air Fryer to 360°F. Place the butter and cheese in two separate bowls.

2. Brush the butter on both sides of the bread. Place the cheese on 2 of the 4 bread pieces.

3. Put together the grilled cheese and add to the Air Fryer cooking basket.

4. Cook until the cheese has melted and is golden brown or for 5 to 7 minutes.

5. Serves and Enjoy

Roti Prata Mini Sausage Rolls

Ready in about 20 min | Servings 4 | Normal

Ingredients:

- 1 packet of Roti Prata
- 10 mini beef sausage

Directions:

1. Slice the Prata into triangles. Roll each sausage in a prata triangle until all are well wrapped.
2. Select bake mode the set the temperature to heat your Air Fryer to 356°F and place the rolls in the fryer basket.
3. Bake them for 15 minutes until crispy, turning the rolls halfway through.
4. Serve and Enjoy

Filo Covered Apple Pie

Ready in about 28 min | Servings 8 | Normal

Ingredients:

- 3 large apples, finely chopped
- 6 teaspoons of sugar
- 6 ounces of melted butter
- 10 sheets of filo pastry
- 2 teaspoons of cinnamon
- 2 teaspoons of flour
- ½ teaspoon of cloves, ground
- ½ teaspoon of nutmeg, ground
- 3 teaspoons of lemon juice

Directions:

1. Mix the apples, flour, lemon juice, cloves, cinnamon, nutmeg, and sugar together in a bowl.
2. Place the filo pastry on a clean surface, unroll and brush gently with butter.
3. Spoon some apple filling and place on the filo sheets about 2" away from the base. Fold the base of the sheet and then a third of the length over the filling. Roll-up the entire filling with the filo sheet to form a triangle shape, brushing the edges with butter.
4. Coat all sides of the filo triangles with the melted butter and sprinkle some sugar on top.
5. Select bake mode the set the temperature to heat your Air Fryer to 320° F and cook the apple pies in batches for 8 minutes, depending on the size. Remove when they appear light brown and crisp.

Serve while warm.

Puff Pastry Banana Rolls

Ready in about 20 min | Servings 3 | Normal

Ingredients:

- 2 puff pastry sheets
- medium-sized bananas, peeled

Directions:

1. Cut the pastry sheets into thin strips—twine two strips to form a cord. Make as many cords as needed.

2. Wind the bananas with the cords until the entire banana is covered with the pastry.

3. Select bake mode the set the temperature to heat your Air Fryer to 356°F and cook the wrapped bananas for about 10 minutes until golden.

Crunchy Sweet Potato Sticks

Ready in about 15 min | Servings 1 | Normal

Ingredients:

- 1 medium-sized sweet potato
- Salt to taste
- 1 teaspoon of coconut oil
- 1 tablespoon of aioli

Directions:

1. Select bake mode the set the temperature to heat your Air Fryer to 200°F.
2. Cut the sweet potato into sticks and toss in the coconut oil.
3. Place the potato sticks into the cooking basket and fry for 10 minutes until they turn crisp.
4. Add the salt and serve with aioli.

Spring Rolls

Ready in about 22 min | Servings 20 | Normal

Ingredients:

- 3 teaspoon of olive oil
- 1 small sized onion, diced
- 2 ounces of Asian noodles
- 1 packet of spring roll wrappers
- 3 cloves of garlic, crushed
- 8 ounces of mixed vegetables
- 1 teaspoon of soy sauce
- 7 ounces of mince
- 6 teaspoons of water

Directions:

1. Put the noodles in hot water, allowing it to soak until soft; drain it, then cut into shorter length.
2. Heat the oil in a skillet, then add the onion, mixed vegetables, mince, and garlic. Cook the mixture until mince is soft, then add soy sauce.
3. Remove from heat and mix with the noodles. Allow standing until the noodles absorb the juices.
4. Place the spring roll wrapper, one after the other, and add the noodle mixture diagonally across. Fold the pointed edge close to the filling over it, then fold the 2 side points together. Brush the last point with water, then roll over the spring roll to seal it.
5. Select bake mode the set the temperature to heat the Air Fryer to 356° F.
6. Coat each roll with oil using a pastry brush in a single layer in Air Fryer to cook for 8 minutes. Cook in batches until all rolls are cooked.

Syrupy Buttered Figs with Mascarpone

Ready in about 15 min | Servings 4 | Normal

Ingredients:

- 2 tablespoons of butter
- 5.2 ounces of mascarpone
- 1 teaspoon of rose water
- 8 figs
- 1½ ounces of maple syrup toasted almonds

Directions:

1. Select bake mode the set the temperature to preheat the Air Fryer to 350°F.
2. Cut the top of the figs vertically and horizontally to form a cross and squeeze the bottom lightly to open.
3. Put a small lump of butter into each fig and place in a dish. Drizzle the maple syrup over the figs.
4. Place the dish into the Air Fryer basket and cook for 5 minutes until soft.
5. Pour the rosewater into the mascarpone and stir. Place a spoonful in each serving and sprinkle the almond on top.

Corn Tortilla Chips

Ready in about 7 min | Servings 3 | Normal

Ingredients:

- 6 teaspoons of vegetable oil
- 8 Corn Tortillas
- Salt to the taste

Directions:

1. Select bake mode the set the temperature to heat the Air Fryer to 390° F.

2. Cut out shapes from the tortillas using a knife. Coat the tortillas with oil using a pastry brush.

3. Put half the tortilla into the fryer basket and cook for 3 minutes. Do the same with the second batch until all the chips are ready.

4. Add the salt and serve hot with a sauce.

Air Fried Banana Chips

Ready in about 30 min | Servings 4 | Normal

Ingredients:

- 3 medium-sized bananas, peeled
- 1 teaspoon of vegetable oil
- ½ teaspoon of Chaat masala seasoning
- ½ teaspoon of Turmeric powder
- 1 teaspoon of salt

Directions:

1. Add about 1½ cups of water to the turmeric powder and a little salt. Slice the bananas into the turmeric mixture to prevent it from getting black by giving it a yellow color. Soak the bananas for 10 minutes and then drain off and dry.

2. Select bake mode the set the temperature to heat your Air Fryer to 356° F for 5 minutes

3. Add the oil to the chips and toss lightly—Fry for 15 minutes in the Air Fryer. Remove from the fryer and add the salt and seasoning. Serve immediately or preserve in an airtight container.

Rosemary Chips

Ready in about 1hr 10 min | Servings 4 | Normal

Ingredients:

- 2 teaspoons of finely chopped rosemary
- 4 russet potatoes
- 3teaspoons of olive oil
- ¼ teaspoon of salt

Directions:

1. Peel potatoes and slice them into thin chips. Soak them in water for 30 minutes, drain and then pat dry with a paper towel.

2. Select bake mode the set the temperature to heat your Air Fryer to about 330° F.

3. Pour the olive oil into the potato chips and toss until all the potatoes are coated.

4. Put the potatoes into the fryer basket and air fry for 30 minutes until golden and crisp. Shake often during cooking to ensure the potatoes are evenly cooked.

4. Remove from fryer, add the rosemary and salt and toss to mix.

Air Fried Crab Sticks

Ready in about 17 min | Servings 1-2 | Normal

Ingredients:

- 1 packet crabsticks, break length-wise and cut into even small pieces
- 2 teaspoon oil
- Cajun or curry seasoning powder (optional)

Directions:

1. Select bake mode the set the temperature to preheat Air Fryer at 325° F for 5 minutes. Place cut and even crab sticks in a bowl and drizzle oil over, tossing well to combine.

2. Air fry until golden brown for 12 minutes. Every few minutes, check to ensure they are cooking evenly.

3. Sprinkle with seasoning if desired.

Bread Rolls with Crisp Potato Stuffing

Ready in about 35 min | Servings 8 | Normal

Ingredients:

- 8 slice bread, white part only
- 5 large potatoes
- 2green chilies, seeded and finely chopped
- 1 small coriander bunch, finely chopped
- 1/2 teaspoon of turmeric
- 2 small onions, finely chopped
- 1/2 teaspoon of mustard seeds
- 2 tablespoons of oil
- 2 sprigs curry leaf
- Salt to the taste

Directions

1. Add the potato, a spoon of salt, and water to a pot. Boil, peel, and mash the potatoes thoroughly.
2. Heat a teaspoon of oil and mustard seeds in a pan. Once they sputter, add the onions and fry until translucent and the curry leaves and add turmeric. Fry and then add the mashed potatoes and salt. Mix well and let it cool.
3. Using your palms, shape the mixture into 8 oval shapes and set aside.
4. Now, trim off the sides of the bread and wet it totally with water. Remove excess water by pressing with your palm.
5. Keeping the wet bread in your palm, place the potato, and roll the bread in a spindle shape. Afterward, seal the edges and ensure that the potato filling is wholly inside the bread.

6. Make all the rolls and brush with oil. Keep aside. Preheat the Air Fryer at 400° F for 8 minutes and brush the basket with some oil before placing the ready rolls.

7. Cook 12-13 minutes until golden crisp. Enjoy with tomato ketchup along with masala chai!

Feta and Onion Bell Pepper Rolls

Ready in about 35 min | Servings 8 | Normal

Ingredients:

- 4 medium-sized bell red and yellow peppers
- 2 tablespoons of finely chopped basil
- 1 green onion, thinly sliced
- 3½ ounces of feta cheese, grated
- 8 toothpicks or tapas forks

Directions:

1. Heat your Air Fryer to 392° F.
2. Place the peppers into the fryer basket and Air Fry for 10 minutes until they are charred to an extent.
3. Mix the feta cheese, basil, and green onions in a bowl and set aside.
4. Bring out the bell peppers and cut them vertically into halves, remove skin and the seeds.
5. Put the feta-onion mixture into each pepper and roll up beginning from the thinner end. Fasten the rolls with a toothpick of a tapas fork and serve.

Spicy Coconut Coated Shrimp

Ready in about 24 min | Servings 4 | Normal

Ingredients:

- 4 ounces of grated coconut
- 16 ounces of large-sized shrimps, peeled, deveined
- 4 ounces of flour
- 2 egg whites, whisked
- 8 tablespoons of breadcrumbs
- ½ teaspoon of salt Zest of 1 small lemon
- Sweet chili sauce
- ½ teaspoon of ground black pepper
- Oil spray

Directions:

1. Mix the breadcrumbs with the zest, pepper, coconut, and salt in a dish and set aside. Season the flour with pepper and salt in a separate dish. Put the eggs in another dish.
2. Heat your Air Fryer to 400°F.
3. Put each shrimp into the flour, then dip into the whisked eggs, and lastly, coat evenly with the breadcrumb mixture.
4. Place the dredged shrimps on a plate and coat with oil using an oil spray.
5. Divide the shrimps into two batches and place the first into the Air Fryer. Cook for 6 minutes until firm. Do the same with the second batch. Turn down the temperature to 340° F and add the first batch to the Air Fryer second. Air fry for 2 more minutes.
6. Best served with sweet chili sauce.

Crispy French Fries

Ready in about 1hr min | Servings 8 | Normal

Ingredients:

- 6 teaspoons of vegetable oil
- 6 medium-sized Irish potatoes

Directions

1. Peel potatoes and slice them into 3" long strips. Soak them in water for 30 minutes, drain, and then dry with a paper towel.
2. Select bake mode the set the temperature to heat your Air Fryer to about 360° F.
3. Pour the oil into the potato strips and toss until thoroughly mixed.
4. Put the potatoes in the fryer basket and cook until golden for 30 minutes, shaking at 10 minutes intervals.

Bacon-Wrapped Shrimp

Ready in about 35 min | Servings 4 | Normal

Ingredients:

- 16 pieces (1¼ pounds) of tiger shrimp, peeled and deveined
- 16 slices (1-pound) of bacon, thinly sliced

Directions:

1. Wrap a slice of bacon around the shrimp completely. Refrigerate the wrapped shrimp for 20minutes.

2. Select bake mode the set the temperature to preheat the Air Fryer to 390° F. Take the shrimp out from the refrigerator and place it in the cooking basket.

3. Cool for 5 to 7 minutes. Drain on a paper towel and serve.

Sage and Onion Stuffing Balls Air-Fryer

Ready in about 18 min | Servings 9 | Normal

Ingredients:

- 3.5 oz of sausage meat
- ½ small onion, peeled and diced
- 1 teaspoon of sage
- ½ teaspoon of garlic puree
- 3 tablespoons of breadcrumbs
- Salt and pepper to the taste

Directions:

1. Combine all ingredients in a bowl and mix well.
2. Form mixture into medium-sized balls and place in the Air Fryer
3. Cook at 350° F for 15 minutes. Serve and enjoy!

Chenjehn

Ready in about 55 min | Servings 2 | Normal

Ingredients:

- 2 lb. of mutton chopped
- 3 onions chopped
- 5 green chilies-roughly chopped
- 1 ½ tablespoons of ginger paste
- 1 teaspoon of garlic paste
- 1 ½ teaspoon of salt
- 3 teaspoon of lemon juice
- 2 teaspoon of garam masala
- 4 tablespoons of chopped coriander
- 3 tablespoons of cream
- 2 tablespoons of coriander powder
- 4 tablespoons of fresh mint (chopped)
- 3 t tablespoons of chopped capsicum
- 2 tablespoons of peanut flour
- 3 eggs

Directions:

1. In a tub, mix dry ingredients. Turn the mixture into a thick paste, and cover the mixture with the cubes of the mutton.

2. Place the eggs in a cup, then apply salt. Dip the cubes into the mixture of the eggs and coat them with seeds and leave them in the fridge for an hour. At 290° F, preheat the Air Fryer for around 5 minutes. Place the kebabs in the basket and make them cook at the same temperature for another 25 minutes. To get a standard cook to switch the kebabs over during the cooking process. Serve with mint chutney kebabs.

Juicy Kebab

Ready in about 30 min | Servings 2 | Normal

Ingredients:

- 2 lb. of chicken breasts cubed
- 3 onions chopped
- 5 green chilies-roughly chopped
- 1 ½ tablespoons of ginger paste
- 1 ½ teaspoon of garlic paste
- 1 ½ teaspoon of salt
- 3 teaspoon of lemon juice
- 2 teaspoon of garam masala
- 4 tablespoons of chopped coriander
- 3 t tablespoons of cream
- 2 tablespoons of coriander powder
- 4 tablespoons. of fresh mint (chopped)
- 3 tablespoons of chopped capsicum
- 2 tablespoons of peanut flour
- 3 eggs

Directions:

1. In a tub, mix dry ingredients. Turn the mixture into a thick paste, and cover the mixture with the chicken cubes.
2. Place the eggs in a cup, then apply salt. Dip the cubes into the mix of the eggs and coat them with sesame seeds and leave them in the fridge for an hour.

3. At 290° F, Preheat the Air Fryer for around 5 minutes. Place the kebabs in the basket and make them cook at the same temperature for another 25 minutes. To get a standard cook to switch the kebabs over during the cooking process. Serve with mint chutney kebabs.

Banana Rolls

Ready about in: 20 min| Serves 3|Easy

Ingredients

- 3 ripe bananas.
- Agaragar prepared in water
- Wheat flour.
- 1 teaspoon baking soda
- 1 teaspoon cinnamon
- 1 teaspoon ginger
- 1/2 teaspoon cloves
- 1/4 teaspoon salt
- 3 large eggs
- 1 cup granulated sugar
- 6 ounces cream cheese, softened
- 5 Tablespoons butter
- 3 cups powdered sugar
- 1 teaspoon vanilla

Directions:

1. Heat your Air Fryer to 375° F,

2. Stir together flour, baking powder, baking soda, cinnamon, ginger, cloves and salt in small bowl

3. Beat eggs and granulated sugar in large mixer bowl until thick

Stir in flour mixture

4. Spread evenly into prepared pan

5. Bake for 10 to 12 minutes or until the top of cake springs back when touched

cool on wire rack

6.While it cools make the frosting: beat cream cheese, butter, and vanilla extract until smooth,

spread frosting over cake

7.Re-roll the cake then wrap in plastic wrap and freeze

8.Remove from the freezer let sit for 10 minutes.

Serve and Enjoy!

Milanese Of Eggplant

Ready about in: 15 min|Serve 2|Easy

Ingredients

- Eggplants
- Chickpea flour
- Traditional flour
- Water
- Breadcrumbs
- Oregano
- Cumin
- Garlic Powder
- Salt

Directions:

1.Mix the cornmeal and chickpea with the water in a bowl.

2.Add cumin, oregano, garlic powder, salt, and mix. In an other container place the breadcrumbs.

3.Peel and cut along the eggplant and set aside. Pass the eggplant one by one through the flour mixture, and then through the breadcrumbs.

4.Place in the Air Fryer and fry for 6 minutes at 390° F.

Serve and Enjoy!

Uruguayan Fried Cakes

Ready about in: 20 min| Serves 2|Normal

Ingredients

- 2 cups of wheat flour.
- 1 ½ teaspoon of baking powder.
- ½ tablespoon of salt.
- 4 tablespoons of oil.
- 1 cup of soy milk
- Agaragar diluted in water
- Lemon zest.
- Sugar.

Directions:

1.2 separate preparation s are made. On the one hand, the agar-agar, oil and ½ cup of milk are mixed.

2.Mix up to foam. On the other hand, the remaining **Ingredients** are mixed.

3.Then mix the 2 mixtures and knead very well, until they stick to the mold.

4.If necessary, more milk is added. Rest for 10 minutes.

5.Make small balls, then stretch.

6.Make a cross cut and put in the Air Fryer for 8 - 12 minutes at 380° F.

7.They bathe with sugar when re moving them from the Fryer.

Serve and Enjoy!

Delicious Malanga

Ready about in: 15 min|Serves 2|Normal

Ingredients

- 3 medium malangas
- 200g vegan cream cheese
- 2 Parsley
- 5 cloves of garlic
- Pepper
- Salt
- Chives

Directions:

1. Peel and grate the raw malanga.

2. Knead with all the ingredients and bring to the Air Fryer for 6 - 10 minutes at 380° F.

3. When the timer reaches 0, then press the cancel button

Serve and Enjoy!

Artichoke Croquettes

Ready about in: 15 min| Serves 2|Normal

Ingredients

- 6 artichoke backgrounds
- ½ kg of soy meat
- 2 slices of bread without skin
- Minced garlic
- 1 cup of flour
- Salt pepper
- 1cdta of sugar
- Lemon juice to taste.

Directions:

1. Hydrate the soy meat for 10 minutes, and then drain well.
2. Salt pepper the meat. Make a mixture of egg, garlic, salt, and pepper.
3. Add bread, lemon juice, sugar and knead well. Mix the artichokes in the previous preparation and then pass them through beaten egg and flour.
4. Place them in the Air Fryer for a period of 6 - 10 minutes at 360° F. Serve adn Enjoy!

Caramelized Bananas

Ready about in: 45 min| Serves 2|Normal

Ingredients

- Ripe bananas.
- 2 tablespoons Brown sugar or brown paper.
- Cinnamon powder.
- water

Directions:

1.Peel the bananas and cut them into pieces.

2.Place them in a small pot with a little oil and sprinkle with the ingredient.

3.Fry in Air Fryer for 35 minutes at 360° F.

Serve and Enjoy!

Banana Pie

Ready about in: 1 hr and 20 min| Serves 3|Easy

Ingredients

- 3 Ripe bananas
- 1/2 cup flour
- 2 eggs
- 2 tablespoons butter
- 3 cups milk
- 2/3 cup white sugar
- 1 teaspoons vanilla
- 1 baked pastry shell
- Water
- 1 teaspoon Salt

Directions:

1.In a saucepan, combine the sugar, flour, and salt. Add milk while stirring.
2.Cook over medium heat for about 3 more minutes, and then remove from the burner.
3.Stir a small quantity of the hot mixture into the beaten egg yolks, Cook for 3 more minutes; remember to keep stirring. Remove the mixture from the stove, and add butter and vanilla.
4.Slice bananas into the cooled baked pastry shell
5.Bake at 350° F for 10 to 18 minutes. Chill for an 50 minutes.

Fried Vegan Milk

Ready about in: 15 min| Serves 3|Easy

Ingredients

- 130 gr of cornstarch
- 1 liter of vegetable milk
- 70 gr of sugar
- Peel of a lemon
- Cinnamon sticks and ground
- Flour
- Vegetable margarine

Directions:

1. Mix ½ liter of vegetable milk in a pot with the lemon peel, the cinnamon stick, and the sugar.
2. Boil for a few minutes. Remove from the fire.
3. In a separate bowl: mix the rest of the vegetable milk with the cornstarch.
4. When finished mixing mix both preparation s and bring to fire for a few minutes.
5. Place the preparation in molds and rest for a few minutes. When cooling, refrigerate.
6. When solidifying the milk, overflow in flour.
7. Place in the Air Fryer at 400° F for 2 minutes. Remove and sprinkle with sugar and ground cinnamon.

Serve up.

Celery Fritters

Ready about in: 20 min| Serves 2|Easy

Ingredients

- 1/3 kg celery.
- 1/3 cup white basil.
- Agar agar diluted in water
- Salt
- 2 cups of soy flour.
- Soy oil.
- A pinch of ginger.

Directions:

1. Wash and peel the celery. Put to parboil that is a little hard, (from 15 to 20min).

2. Chop the basil finely. Whisk the egg. Stir the celery and mix with basil, agar-agar, salt, and ginger to taste. Knead well and form balls. Roll them in the soy flour.

3. Take them to the Air Fryer at 380° F, for 8 - 12 minutes.

4. Serve up decorated with branches of parsley or basil to taste.

Vegan Donuts

Ready about in: 25 min| Serves 2|Easy

Ingredients

- 120 g of vegetable drink
- 50 g of vegan margarine.
- 2 tablespoons of sunflower oil
- The zest of 1 lemon.
- 250 g whole wheat flour.
- 3 teaspoon fresh yeast
- ½ teaspoon of salt
- 50 g of muscovite sugar.

Directions:

1. First, melt the margarine in a small saucepan over medium heat.
2. Add the vegetable drink and the sun flower oil. Sift all the dry ingredients in a bowl.
3. Add the lemon zest and integrate with the other ingredients. Make the shape of a volcano and integrate the liquid in the center of the mixture of the dry ones little by little with a fork.
4. When it is moldable, take it out to the table, knead it and take pieces of the dough. Stretch and cut circularly. Make a hole in the center.
5. Set the Air Fryer at 15 - 20 minutes at 260º F.
6. Put the donuts Remove and glaze with dark chocolate, sugar or whatever you prefer.

Andes Cakes

Ready about in: 30 min| Serves 2|Easy

Ingredients

- Flour all use.
- 1 cup of water.
- 1 teaspoon salt.
- 100 g of shortening.
- Cold rice
- Vegetable stew

Directions:

Dough:

1. Place the dough in a bowl; place the warm water, butter, and salt.

2. Knead little, make the dough hard. Let stand for 10 minutes. After this time, stretch with a roller and cut circles.

3. Mix the cold rice and the vegetable stew to taste. Place the dough circles by teaspoons with a brush, moisten the edges and close.

4. Puncture with a stick and fry in the Air Fryer for 8 - 15 minutes at 360° F.

5. When the timer reaches 0, then press the cancel button

Serve and Enjoy!

Eggplant with Garlic

Ready about in: 15 min| Serves 2|Easy

Ingredients

- 2 eggplants
- 6 cloves of garlic
- 2 tablespoon olive oil
- 1 bay leaf
- Salt
- Pepper.

Directions:

1. Peel the eggplants, leave them a few minutes with water and salt to expel the bitter, and then drain very well.

2. Cut them in 4 lengthways, remove the seeds and cut each quarter into 3mm strips. Crush garlic cloves and integrate all the ingredients.

3. Place in the Air Fryer at 360° F for 8 minutes.

4. Watch the cooking half the time flips.

Serve and Enjoy|

Apple Fritters

Ready about in: 20 min| Serves 2|Easy

Ingredients

- 2 large apples
- 200g of flour
- Salt
- A ¼ liter of cider or beer
- 1 teaspoon olive oil
- Sugar

Directions:

1. First, peel the apples and remove the seeds. Cut into rings and sprinkle sugar.

2. Add the flour in a bowl and add salt, oil, and beer. Mix sprinkle the apples in the mixture and place them in the Air Fryer tray with butter paper.

3. Fry for 10 - 15 minutes at 360° F.

4. Add sugar and Serve up hot.

Cinammon Apples

Ready about in: 15 min| Serves 2|Easy

Ingredients

- 2 apples
- ⅔ cups cornstarch
- 1 spoon of sugar
- ⅛ teaspoon of cinnamon
- ½ cup of caramel sauce

Directions:

1. Peel and cut the apples. Mix with the cornstarch.
2. Fry in the Air Fryer for 6 minutes at 360° F.
3. When the timer reaches 0, then press the cancel button
4. Flip to be cooked on both sides.
5. Spray cinnamon and sugar when serving.

Fried Tofu

Ready about in: 15 min| Serve 2|Easy

Ingredients

- Extra Firm Tofu
- Soy sauce
- Cornstarch
- 1 pinch Chive
- 2 teaspoons vegetable oil

Directions:

1. First, remove the liquid from the tofu by pressing it. Place it on absorbent paper.

2. Cut into long squares or strips. Flour well in the cornstarch.

3. Add to the Air Fryer and fry for 8 - 10 minutes at 380° F.

4. Meanwhile, cut the chives into strips. Add tofu and continue frying. Remove and Serve up with soy sauce.

Vegan French Toast with Oregano

Ready about in: 15 min| Serves 2|Easy

Ingredients

- Cornstarch
- 250g of leavening flour
- 250g of Wheat germ
- Salt.
- Oregano.
- Pepper to taste
- 1 grated carrot
- 7 tablespoons of olive oil
- 1 glass of water

Directions:

1. Place the dry ingredients in a bowl and mix with the wet ingredients.

2. Add the grated carrot and mix. Place a little oil in the Air Fryer tray to avoid sticking.

3. Place a portion of the mixture and Fry at 390° F for 5 minutes, or until golden brown.

4. Serve up alone or sprinkled with sugar.

Vegan Chips

Ready about in: 15 min| Serve 2|Easy

Ingredients

- 1 cucumber
- 1 clove garlic
- 1 lemon
- 350g of vegan yogurt
- 2 tablespoon of olive oil
- Salt
- Pepper to taste
- 1 sprig of parsley to decorate
- 1 yucca
- 1 sweet potato
- 1 beet
- 1 carrot

Directions:

1. Peel the cucumber and cut it in half lengthwise. Remove the seeds and grate.
2. Add a pinch of salt and remove the moisture. Process the cucumber, garlic, yogurt, lemon juice, olive oil and salt and pepper. Peel and cut the tubers into thin slices.
3. Place in the Air Fryer and fry at 380° F for 3 - 5 minutes or until crispy.
4. Sprinkle with salt and Serve up accompanied by cucumber cream.

Vegetarian Pizza

Ready about in: 55 min| Serves 4|Normal

Ingredients

- 200 gr of wheat flour
- 2 gr of yeast
- 1 pinch of salt
- 1 pinch of sugar
- Oregano to taste
- 2 olive oil
- 1 grated carrot
- Creamy vegan cheese
- Olives of your choice
- 3 slices of sliced red paprika
- Spices to taste
- Grated ginger
- 1 pinch of grated vegan cheese

Directions:

1.In a bowl, add the flour together with the yeast, salt, sugar, oregano and oil in a bowl.

2.Add little by little the warm water. Mix until the dough is solid. Knead until it forms a bun that does not stick, let it rest for more than half an hour.

3.Paint the mold of the Air Fryer with olive oil. Place the dough stretched to taste.

4.Fry at 260° F for 10 minutes or until light. Fry for 5 more minutes until golden brown. Add the cream cheese until it melts.

5.Finally, add the carrot, olives, paprika, ginger and grated cheese.

6.Fry for 2 - 3 minutes if you want to cook the vegetables.

www.ingramcontent.com/pod-product-compliance
Lightning Source LLC
Chambersburg PA
CBHW070938080526
44589CB00013B/1563